Harry D. Strunk
1892-1960

Service is the Rent We Pay for the Space We Occupy in this World

by
Allen D. Strunk

Bloomington, IN authorHOUSE® Milton Keynes, UK

AuthorHouse™
1663 Liberty Drive, Suite 200
Bloomington, IN 47403
www.authorhouse.com
Phone: 1-800-839-8640

AuthorHouse™ UK Ltd.
500 Avebury Boulevard
Central Milton Keynes, MK9 2BE
www.authorhouse.co.uk
Phone: 08001974150

This is a reprint from the McCook Daily Gazette Centennial Edition 1882-1982.

© 2007 Allen D. Strunk. All rights reserved.

No part of this book may be reproduced, stored in a retrieval system, or transmitted by any means without the written permission of the author.

First published by AuthorHouse 12/3/2007

ISBN: 978-1-4259-8254-6 (sc)

Printed in the United States of America
Bloomington, Indiana

This book is printed on acid-free paper.

It was a warm summer afternoon in the early 1940s when Harry D. Strunk entered the large, white two-story home at 611 Norris Avenue which had been converted into the McCook Elks Lodge a few decades before.

Hardly a day passed that the editor-publisher didn't visit the Elks home which was a center of card playing, drinking and kibitzing for the community's railroaders, farmers, business and professional men and – during the war – for the more affluent of the some 5,000 plus troops stationed at the Army Air Base nine miles north of McCook.

Strunk was a charter member of the organization and, in later years, divided his time almost equally between the Elks Lodge and his newspaper office two blocks to the south.

On this day, he had hardly sat down at the bar and ordered a drink when he was verbally accosted by an Army captain who also frequented the Elks and who had just recently been arrested for driving while under the influence of alcohol. To make matters worse, the captain was responsible for the motor pool operation at the base and had consequently received an appropriate reprimand.

On spotting Strunk, the captain unloaded his embarrassment and frustration.

"Here I am out here in this God-forsaken place serving my country … I stop for a cool beer … and what do your police do?

"And, you, you put it all over your lousy newspaper," the captain complained.

The verbal abuse went on for some time and finally Strunk asked:

"Just where was it in the paper?"

"Well hell, it was right there where everyone could see it!"

"But was it on the front page?" Strunk asked.

"No, but damn it, everyone saw it."

"Well," replied Strunk, "if you'd have been a colonel or general or someone important, we would have put it on the front page!"

That was the quick-witted editor who was honored in mid 1952 when the Congress of the United States broke precedent and named a federally constructed Bureau of Reclamation project for a living man.

By a unanimous vote, the U.S. Senate passed S103 designating the water behind the recently constructed Medicine Creek Dam, north of Cambridge, to be known as Harry Strunk Lake in honor of the driving force behind the flood control and reclamation development in Southwest Nebraska, Northwest Kansas and the edge of Eastern Colorado.

The senate action was guided by Sens. Fred Seaton of Hastings and Hugh Butler of Cambridge. The latter died a short time later and earned similar name-honor after his death with the completion of Red Willow Dam north of McCook.

Nebraska Third District Representative Carl Curtis of Minden, who later advanced to the U.S. Senate, piloted an accompanying name-honoring bill through the House of Representatives.

"It gives me real pleasure to take this opportunity to pay tribute to a great leader in the cause of reclamation in Southwest Nebraska, my good friend Harry Strunk of McCook, Nebraska," Sen. Butler said in introducing the legislation.

"The naming of this reservoir after Harry Strunk is but a small measure of the appreciation felt by all the people of the valley for his leadership. I am sure that the decision to do him this honor will meet the virtually unanimous support of the people there.

"The movement to bring reclamation to the Republican River Valley in Nebraska got its real start as a result of the drought years of the 30s and the disastrous flood which swept down the valley in 1935.

"Harry Strunk welded the people of the valley into a unified group to press for extension of federal reclamation and flood control programs to the valley.

"For many years, it was a long, uphill campaign, but Harry Strunk and his supporters never lost faith. Just when their plans seemed to the point of bearing fruit, WWII came along and put an end to all construction. But Harry Strunk kept the movement going and used the time to good advantage in developing plans and broadening support for the program. Congressional authorization for a program of development of the water resources of the valley was secured near the end of the war. As soon as hostilities were concluded, the federal government was ready to go ahead.

"I believe it is altogether fitting that this reservoir on Medicine Creek be named in honor of Harry Strunk," Sen. Butler told the Senate.

The action, which had also been endorsed by the Interior Department and the Bureau of the Budget, was signed by President Harry S. Truman and became a law that broke precedent in that it was believed to have been only the second time in American history that the water behind a federally constructed dam was named in honor of a living person.

The other such incident was the renaming of Boulder Dam in Nevada in honor of former President Herbert Hoover, who was still living when the name change occurred.

Although the federal policy has been relaxed in recent years, it apparently was based on sound judgment since even though admirers of Harry Strunk contended he had accomplished more for his area than any other person ever, the lake naming was not without challenge.

While the Harry Strunk Lake naming was under consideration, Raymond A. McConnell Jr., editor of the Nebraska State Journal (later to become the Lincoln Journal) wrote editorially:

"Rep. Carl Curtis' effort to have Medicine Creek Reservoir renamed in honor of Harry Strunk, publisher of the McCook Daily Gazette, raises the question of whether there might not be worked out some system, for future reservoirs, of names with both beauty and historical meaning – not that Strunk isn't a beautiful name to people named Strunk."

The Strunk naming criticism wasn't limited to Nebraska and even made the national press when George Dixon of the Washington Times Herald (since discontinued) wrote:

"Sen. Hugh Butler of Nebraska apparently has no ear for romantic-sounding names. He has just introduced a bill to change the name of Nebraska's Medicine Creek Reservoir to Harry Strunk Lake."

McConnell, having been on the Nebraska scene for some time, should have known his editorial remarks would trigger a response, but the editorial writer in the nation's capital apparently didn't know that Strunk was a newspaperman battle-scarred from some 40 years of editorial dueling. Nor did perhaps either of them know of Strunk's eagerness to jump into the middle of any disagreement, and his unbelievable determination to win and his skill of strategy which had built a daily newspaper amongst fierce competition.

If they weren't aware they were unleashing a wildcat when they attacked the lake naming, they found out shortly as Strunk defended his honor in a front page editorial in the GAZETTE Jan. 29, 1951.

The editorial read in part:

> As far as Harry Strunk is concerned, you fellows ought to work out a system of naming the reservoirs of this country and in that process it would give me great pleasure if either of your names were ever mentioned as a part of the program which has been built over a period of

years before you boys started in the newspaper business.

Through this entire program there has been a lack of interest on the part of metropolitan newspapers to see to it that the resources of this country are conserved and preserved for the benefit of the people … and now that this job is partially completed, I find apparently a jealousy as to what name should be applied to a dam or a reservoir.

As far as I am concerned, it makes no difference to me and I don't think to our organization, as to what name is placed on any dam or any reservoir in the Republican Valley, so long as the devastation is stopped and these waters are used to the benefit of the people and McConnell, you can have it, we will name it "McConnell Reservoir" and "McConnell Dam" … if you can show me or our people where you had one damn thing to do with the development of this country.

It is small-town stuff, even in the capital of the state to write your kind of stuff when you criticize the work of men who have been spending a lifetime to save and develop such resources as your Salt Creek in Lincoln … where a columnist and editor are absolutely responsible for a lack of cooperation between the federal agencies and your own people to stop the devastation which took place in your community and your territory during the past year ... where in the hell were you, "Mac," during all these years and where did you get so smart to tell everyone off as to how in the world they could continue to develop this state and name a dam or reservoir.

There has always been the tendency of too many criticizing the program which has as its objective the control and utilization of the waste waters of this country ... take a look at the Salt Creek, take a look at your Loups, the Plattes, and Central Valley ... take a look at all the waste water which flows through Nebraska to create destruction without any return ... and then add to your interest power and navigation, transportation and come out with an open statement as to what you think we should start from now, after 10 years of Nebraska standing first in the 17 reclamation states in development.

Believe me, it is our desire to build more reservoirs and dams, regardless of any distinction which any man might enjoy in the work which has been done in which you have not been a part ... so, Raymond, you go ahead, you name the reservoirs and as far as I am concerned, so long as this program continues, we in this part of the country will be happy.

When the flood waters of Salt Creek are stopped and controlled, I will be the one who will subscribe to naming the dam after Raymond A. McConnell, Jr.

Approximately a year and a half later after the name legislation had become law and in a less emotional editorial, Strunk wrote in part:

In acceptance of this fine tribute paid to me by the Congress of the United States and the President, I wish to distribute the honors among the others who have been faithful and determined throughout the years of development and who still stand, I think, staunchly behind the theory on which this organization was formed ... that this job will not be completed until every drop of water that falls in this drainage basin is controlled and utilized for the benefit of the greatest number of people.

Such battles were nothing new for Harry Strunk who had already spent some 40 years in the newspaper world, most of it in keen competition in a market too small to support the number of publications vying for the limited readers and small advertising budgets.

With only an eighth grade education, Strunk had entered the newspaper business at 14, was a publisher at age 16, a shop foreman responsible for 10 hand-typesetting employees at age 17 and opened the Red Willow County Gazette in 1911 at the age of 19.

McCook's population was only about 4,000 in 1911 when Strunk founded the Red Willow County Gazette in the face of two established weekly newspapers in McCook and six in the county.

The Red Willow County Gazette was started one-up on the competition in that it printed twice weekly while both the Republican and Tribune came out only once each per week. Establishment of the new publication took decades of hard work, long hours and little profit. Strunk observed years later that he would likely never have succeeded if the Tribune had gone daily when the GAZETTE began. The Tribune eventually went semi-weekly and later tri-weekly while the Republican (later the Advertiser which dropped news content and later became the Early Bird Town and Country Advertiser) remained weekly in frequency.

Strunk had a partner in the new venture but for only the first issue. On the day of the second issue the partner—Burris Stewart—apparently depressed over the additional debt and family problems, committed suicide.

Strunk carried on with the new publication, and married Arlene Allen a year later. She became a mainstay in the success of the operation for the next 70 years serving as typesetter, reporter, society editor and bookkeeper at various times.

Strunk and Stewart were both printers working for Frank M. Kimmell at the Tribune when they left to open their own newspaper. Kimmell's bitterness never ended. It became an obsession with him and for years he carried on a running editorial battle as he lambasted Strunk's ability, mentality, character and even his honesty.

The feud at one point became so intense that A. Barnett, respected as the community's leading builder and banker, called a meeting of community leaders at which he asked Strunk to end the open newspaper war.

Strunk told the "City Fathers" he would let up as soon as they could convince Kimmell to do likewise but the feud continued. It only dissipated after the GAZETTE went daily in 1924 and time found Kimmell aging and mellowing. Even though the weekly editorial attacks slowed down in later years, the tension and competition remained fierce until the late 1920s when the elderly Kimmell died. His wife sold the paper about four years later to M. C. Smith who operated it until June 20, 1936, when it was sold to the GAZETTE thus ending McCook's first newspaper which had been founded in 1882.

In the constant editorial barrage, Kimmell would refer to Strunk by several names. The most common title was "Rastus Ramrod," apparently in reference to Strunk's tall, lean frame, and the "Boy Editor," in reference to his youth.

For many years, Kimmell rarely published without some comment about "Rastus Ramrod" or the "Boy Editor." Whether it was short in content, or a full scale attack, the Tribune editor seemed possessed to hurl some type of sting to which Strunk more often than not replied.

A typical editorial remark from the educated Kimmell, who acquired a strong vocabulary, was when he wrote:

> When Rastus Ramrod (who hasn't put it back) takes his gory snickersnee in hand and inglorious writes people of the local map – socially and financially – he is sumpin' fierce – as well as casually monstrously amusing, and calls to mind stunts of the elongated pole-climbing simian who sat down in a can of luminous paint before one of his ascents unmindful or witless of his mounting merriment.

Kimmell's "who-hasn't-put-it-back" phrase was the root of his greatest attack against Strunk. Kimmell contended Strunk had stolen $200 from the taxpayers in 1915 by virtue of bidding for the publication of the county tax delinquency list at a figure below the rate established by law.

When finding himself in financial trouble later in the year, Strunk returned to the county commissioners, explained his crisis and asked if they could see their way clear to pay the additional amount allowed by law. The commissioners agreed and Strunk was paid the additional $200 which kept his publication afloat.

In the year that followed, the Tribune leveled a near constant attack of "put the $200 back."

In January of 1916 after Strunk won the legal publication status voted by the county commissioners, he wrote an editorial under the heading "With Everything Fixed – How Lovely" in which he described how the McCook Tribune and the Indianola Reporter planned to split the county legals and expected to freeze out the GAZETTE. Strunk further used the occasion to defend his honesty and pose the question of why would the county do business with him again if he weren't honest?

On Jan. 13, 1916 he wrote:

> Tuesday afternoon, Jan. 11, was a wonderful day for the printing fraternity of Red Willow County. It was a day of premeditation, and the boys all wore a smile, that is all but the Boy Editor of the GAZETTE, who was not allowed to take part in the "fixing of things."
>
> Consequently, when the Boy Editor arose from his cot on the morning of Tuesday last, he did so under a deep spell of the blues. It was a dreadful moment, to know that one's brother publishers had forsaken him and cast him from the fraternity, an organization as strong as the rocks of ages and as faithful as the Sons of Israel, all for the sake of the fact that the GAZETTE honestly collected $200 from the county last year

for printing the delinquent tax list, and did not split it with certain ones.

Tuesday was the big event at the Court House when the County Commissioners handed out the printing supplies for the coming year.

Brother Pontius mounted the early morning train from Indianola and traveled to the county seat.

At about twenty minutes of twelve o'clock noon, Brother Kimmell trotted from his sanctum to the Court House smiling and bowing to the pedestrians as he slipped and tripped up the hill with a cold north wind smiting him in the face.

And the Boy Editor from one corner of his club room sat by the sizzling radiator and watched the fun.

In one hand Mr. Kimmell carried several envelopes labeled "Proposed for County Printing" and parties who passed down the west side of Main Avenue from the Court House to the Temple Theater corner, between 11:30 and 11:35, will testify to the scene of Editors Kimmell and Pontius standing in the cold with the north wind whistling thru their whiskers at the rate of about fifty miles an hour, discussing "just what the commissioners would do" when they opened the proposals for bids, and "how everything had been fixed so lovely" and "the effect the publicity would have about that $200." It must have been a grand moment for these two diplomats, to know that through their ability and keen way of manipulating things, that "everything was alright" and the goose hung high and wide above the reach of Boy Editor, the repudiator.

With this remark: "I don't see how they can possibly award him any part," Mr. Kimmell and Mr. Pontius separated, the former continuing his most important journey to the Court House, where he filed with the County Clerk Dutcher his "proposals for printing" that were to start a new era in the county printing field.

At the exact minute of 11:56 he, in company with Commissioner Sughroue, came from the Court House and proceeded down the street.

With everything fixed the noon meal must have tasted more delicious than ever before, the world must have been bright and the end of a perfect day in sight.

With everything fixed, (unbeknown to the County Commissioners) the officials took their seats promptly at two o'clock in the afternoon as per the schedule advertised.

One by one the envelopes were opened and the contents spread upon the minutes until none was left but those from the GAZETTE.

Everything was fixed alright enough, and high too. And so arranged that each would get a portion without a smell offered the GAZETTE.

However, when the blue envelopes were opened and Clerk Dutcher began penciling the prices and stipulations on the minutes, a cloud of gloom fell over the room. Only Pontius could muster up courage enough to stand before the board and protest. His arguing on various points of law and proving his ignorance disgusted even his followers.

Finally with "I make a motion that all county printing be allowed the Red Willow County Gazette" and that it be designated as the "official county paper," like a whipped pup Pontius stagger to his feet with a sob and waggled from the room.

You might guess the smile of satisfaction which lightened the countenance of the Boy Editor, for it was truly a victorious moment for him. All the county printing, to the repudiator, in spite of the fact, as quoted from the Tribune and Reporter, he "absolutely stole $200 from the county" and "committed the only petty raid on the county treasure in the past forty years."

Right here, the editor would like to ask the dear reader to consider these past charges so fiercely made by the Tribune and the Reporter.

Is it possible one could make "a petty raid on the county treasury" without being brought before law and justice?

If the Boy Editor did "steal $200 from the county," why did these gentlemen not see to it that the laws were enforced, instead of muttering to themselves through the columns of their newspapers?

If the Boy Editor "stole $200 from the county" why are not the County Sheriff, the County Attorney, the County Treasurer and Clerk, bound by oath to protect the moneys of the county, and why, I say, did they not protect?

And finally, why would the County Commissioners, the following year allow ALL the printing to a newspaper boy that would perpetrate such a steal on the county?

It appears to the editor that any fair minded person could see the boycott game which has been going on for the past year, and might realize the why and wherefore.

The Red Willow County Gazette is the official paper of Red Willow County—and the Boy Editor is proud of this fact. It is indeed consoling to know that one is not judged by his enemies.

The Red Willow County Gazette is in a better position than ever before to serve its readers and during the next twelve months will contain all legal notices and official publications of this county.

"Everything is fixed, alright" and if you don't believe it, just ask Mr. Kimmell or Pontius.

A fair relation with your own business well manipulated brings results that are well worth the most prosperous business man.

The legal printing victory for Strunk in 1916 didn't end the Kimmell bombardment nor the "put-it-back" theme. Into the following decade the senior editor stabbed at the "Boy Editor" in attacks that didn't fully appear to make sense to the average reader.

A typical blast was tied to a claim by Strunk of having set a travel time record in a trip from McCook to Colorado Springs which took 10 hours 30 minutes.

The Tribune editor wrote:

> The Boy Editor evidently acquired a bad case of dyspepsia or colic during his recent hobnobbing with the millionaires in the Colorado Springs neighborhood and breaking speed records with his

six cylinder over the "Little England" highways during his recent vacation.

No sooner had the "big boss" resumed his accustomed place in the semi-weekly sewer before his filthy habit of blackguarding the editor of the Tribune became active.

The basis of Mr. Hasn't-Put-Back's slimy overflow is the declination of an employee of the Tribune to be a party to a loan or sale of paper to an employee of the sewer when it was only necessary to make the required financial arrangements with the Burlington company to get an ample supply of their own from the depot. So much for that silly spasm.

The reference to the financial affairs of the Tribune was libelous and cowardly and for the most part false. The Tribune is not familiar with the C.O.D system of securing supplies.

And finally, the ghoulish reference to his former and lamented partner and villainous suggestion of dirty stories alleged to have been recited on the streets by this writer, in the connection, brands the county contract violator as a liar whom the sanctity of the grave of a mourned partner does not deter or shame.

Another of Strunk's heated and long battles pitted him against the highly influential U.S. Sen. George W. Norris, a

Southwest Nebraska lawyer-judge who was McCook's most famous son.

Sen. Norris is given credit for creating Nebraska's non-partisan one-house legislature, introducing the Lame Duck Amendment, and playing a key role in creating public power in Nebraska as well as giving birth to rural electrification and the Tennessee Valley Authority.

Grandson

"Move over Gramps, I'll edit it!" That is what Harry Strunk's first of six grandchildren, Korvin Powell, might have said when the photographer caught the two-year-old "cowboy" visiting his grandad.

For nearly three decades of Norris' political life, Strunk had been a Norris fan and generally supported the "Gentle Knight."

But the two split sharply after Strunk was denied Norris' help in construction of dams to protect the upper Republican River Valley and its tributaries.

Strunk contended flood control and irrigation should be the major objectives while Sen. Norris failed to support the local effort forming in Southwest Nebraska under the editorial leadership of Strunk and the GAZETTE. Sen. Norris further accused Strunk of being in sympathy with the profit-motivated electric power interests.

With Victor Westermark of Benkleman and later district judge at McCook, as president, and Strunk as chairman, some 30 communities in Southwest Nebraska and Northwest Kansas had banned together in 1928 to form the Twin Valley Association of Commercial Clubs with the purpose of controlling the Frenchman and Republican Rivers and tributaries.

Strunk wrote the senator to determine specifically where he stood in support of the newly formed organization and received a Dec. 14, 1929 letter in response.

In six single-spaced typewritten pages, the senator accused Strunk of having misrepresented the senator's viewpoint on the water issue and accused Strunk of being part of the "Power Trust."

"You have recently, very recently, been converted to the Power Trust idea. You want this same monopoly which has tried to enter the back door of our public schools and poison the minds of our children, which has secretly gone into business organizations and commercial clubs and has even tried to contaminate the minds of Boy Scout organizations, which has tried to control legislators, governors and commissioners, and which has even tried to buy seats in the U.S. Senate, to have control of the electricity which results as a by-product from the expenditure of the people's money in the construction of these storage dams. You want to give this Trust the property belonging to the people and let it have the privilege of selling it back to the people at exorbitant profits. I am opposed to this, and that is where our paths diverge."

"There can be but one reason," Sen. Norris stated in another part of his letter adding, "the sinister activities of the Power Trust have reached you."

"Do you expect to have heavy contracts for advertising from the Power Trust or is there some other consideration," he further charged.

Strunk was dumbfounded over the Power Trust "sell-out" charge. What he wanted was for the powerful senator to use his prestige to open the Washington doors so that dam and irrigation construction would be provided in the Republican Valley. If hydro-electric power could be a part of that development, fine but Strunk didn't want the projects delayed further while power interests fought.

The "sell-out" charge set off Strunk and he quickly challenged the senator to back up that allegation.

Noting that Sen. Norris would return to Nebraska to clarify the issue at a meeting planned in Minden in January 1930, Strunk wrote an editorial Dec. 28, 1929 denying the "sell-out" charge:

"We would like to call attention to the fact that during the year now coming to a close, this newspaper started and led a local attack upon the Nebraska Light and Power Company, which resulted in a reduction in local rates amounting to approximately $30,000 annually to consumers. The Nebraska Light and Power Company is listed by Sen. Norris as a unit of the Power Trust.

"We would call attention to the fact that never has this newspaper indicated complete satisfaction in the settlement that was negotiated last summer by the McCook City Council with the light and power company."

Speaking at Minden Jan. 3, 1930, Sen. Norris maintained his general support of flood control and irrigation but dwelt on the power side.

"You will find the Power Trust will have no objection to your spending money for flood control, navigation and irrigation," the senator said, "but when you begin to develop power you will find that the Power Trust will shout "'That is ours'!"

After pointing out the advantages that would accrue to the public from government production of cheap electricity, Sen. Norris said:

"To allow this fourth great element of the flood control program to slip into other hands would be unpatriotic, it would be an economic loss, it would be crazy.

"I'd rather suffer disaster," he said, "than to see the government build dams for flood control, irrigation and navigation and turn the benefits in hydro-electric development over to the power people."

Sen. Norris had come back to Nebraska — answered charges and hurled charges, but nothing had really changed. He still hadn't agreed to lift a finger to help the newly formed organization of which Harry Strunk was to later become its long time president.

Twin Valley Association of Commercial Clubs President Victor Westermark made the following comment after the Minden session:

"While the senator outlined the four-fold plan or purpose of flood control, irrigation, navigation and development of electric power, he failed to show that he would take any initial leadership in getting the cooperation of the senators and representatives and in formulating plans that would bring about the necessary congressional action desired by this territory.

"In other works, if the development of electricity was not a part of the program, the main objective of the move – flood control and irrigation – would be sacrificed."

United Press reported the senator retracted his "sell-out" charge against Strunk who was quoted as saying he (Strunk) saw little likelihood of reconciliation.

"If the senator still feels that the power issue is paramount in this controversy on flood control, irrigation and navigation, he is not only going to force this paper to look elsewhere for representation in the U.S. Senate for its irrigation program, but is going to force many other friends to desert him," the editor was quoted as saying.

With the bitterness set, Stunk went to work in support of the man who was to be Sen. Norris' 1930 opponent, Gilbert Hitchcock, founder and president of the Omaha World-Herald.

However as the year wore on, Strunk predicted in an Oct. 27, 1930 letter to one of Hitchock's aides that Hitchcock would not carry Red Willow County.

"In fact, I don't believe he will carry many counties in this territory. I do look for him to run Norris close in all of them. Hitchcock has failed to touch the issue out here that is the closest to the hearts of the people, and that is flood control and irrigation.

"In his talks he has left the Republican Valley out, speaking entirely of the Platte. Of course, the thinking people realize that the Platte is larger than the Republican and that it should and will come first for consideration, nevertheless, as Norris refused to cooperate with the people out there it is the thing that has driven many away from him (Norris) and should be used here above any other argument for his retirement.

"Tell him to hit more on flood control and conservation of the water resources and to use Norris' refusal to cooperate with his hometown people on this movement – and not to forget ALL rivers of the state when he does mention this point," Strunk concluded.

Sen. Norris was re-elected by a wide state margin of more than 190,000 to about 139,000 and carried Red Willow County 2,848 to 1,094. It was not until 1942 that the long time political figure was retired and that was in a defeat to Kenneth Wherry, a friend of Strunk's since childhood at Pawnee City. From the day of Wherry's election, the man who rose to become majority whip, was a staunch supporter of reclamation development and a great help to Strunk in developing Southwest Nebraska.

In the immediate years that followed, as Southwest Nebraska and the Middle West became preoccupied with the Dust Bowl and the nation was turned upside down by the Great Depression, flood control fell into the background. The Twin Valley Association became inactive and everyone seemed to conclude no development was coming for the Republican Valley – that is, everyone except Harry D. Strunk who kept regular editorials on the subject before his readers.

In the middle of the Depression and the Dust Bowl days came the great flood of 1935 that swept the valley causing millions of dollars in destruction and claiming some 113 lives. Still nothing in the way of dam construction was insight and all the time Sen. Norris was busy developing the Tennessee Valley with dams, irrigation and lots of hydro-electric power.

Then in 1940 the Nebraska senator waved his hand in support of an Army Engineer project on the Republican River.

Where? At Republican City, nearly 80 miles downstream from McCook.

During the 1929-30 clash, the news media reported the split between the longtime friends. Now in 1940, the Omaha World Herald News Service described Strunk as a longtime foe of Sen. Norris and noted Strunk wrote a front-page editorial charging the senator with "reversing himself and insulting Valley friends."

"This is not the first time he has insulted the folks back home," Strunk wrote. "Nor is it the first time he has advocated and worked for water conservation and flood control in other places.

"The people of the upper Republican Valley are not, and have not yet started a fight against any project," Strunk wrote. "What they have done is to question building any one dam and reservoir any one place."

The Strunk-Norris clash was again in the news with editors across the state offering comments. One such editorial that gave a fairly accurate overview came from the Norfolk Daily News under the title: Norris and the Home folk. It read:

> Sen. Norris and the good folks of his hometown are at outs again.
>
> The senator has abandoned his friends at the Southwest corner of the state and has thrown in with the Army Engineers, on the important matter of controlling and using the waters of the Republican River.

The residents of the territory that was devastated by the flood of a few years ago have united behind a project for a series of dams on the tributaries of the Republican, which would impound the water and conserve it for irrigation of thirsty crops as far west as the Nebraska-Colorado line.

Sen. Norris evidently agreed with this plan, but the Army Engineers, with their minds on the protection of the lower sections of the river in Kansas, decided the solution was the building of one huge dam near Republican City, 75 or 80 miles east of McCook and nearly 150 miles east of where the Republican crosses into Nebraska.

Now Sen. Norris announces that he will support the engineers' scheme, although it will give no protection to the district that suffered worst in the big flood and will afford no water for the irrigation of four counties west of Republican City.

The people of the Valley are realistic enough to know that if Uncle Sam spends $22 million on the Republican City project, he will never let go of any more money for the section that really needs the protection and the water.

But the senator calls his neighbors "narrow minded" for opposing this use of the money. His neighbors feel that this is an "insult" which they resent.

As for the rest of us who look on from the sidelines, the controversy confirms our view that the federal government is not primarily interested in using Nebraska waters for irrigation purposes, which is the most valuable use to which they could be put. And the suspicion that Sen. Norris is not much concerned with irrigation seems to be strengthened by his new stand.

But Harry D. Strunk didn't let down, and the upstream projects did materialize. The Republican Valley Conservation Association was formed in 1940 with Strunk as its president and it resulted in the construction of six man-made reservoirs above Republican City in Southwest Nebraska, Northwest Kansas and Eastern Colorado in the following 20 years.

The structures not only prevent future flooding but irrigated approximately 67,000 acres. None of them include hydro-electric power. Sen. Norris died Sept. 3, 1944 just as the first construction was to begin. He had spent 10 years in the House of Representatives and 30 years in the Senate.

Sen. Norris couldn't or didn't really see the value of the upstream reclamation but time may prove his hydro-electric argument significant as energy grows ever more dear. Strunk may have sensed this also since he rose to object when in 1957 Sen. Norris' name was omitted from the senate committee selection of the five greatest senators of all time.

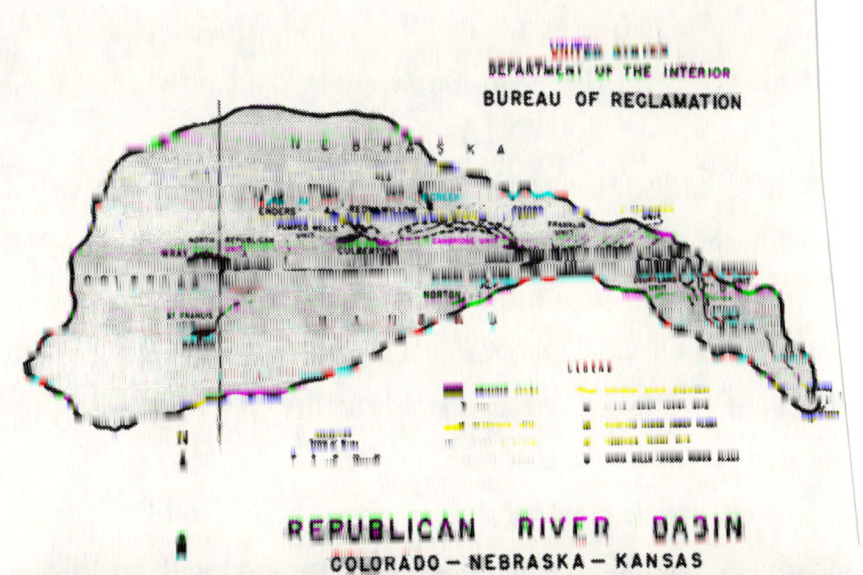

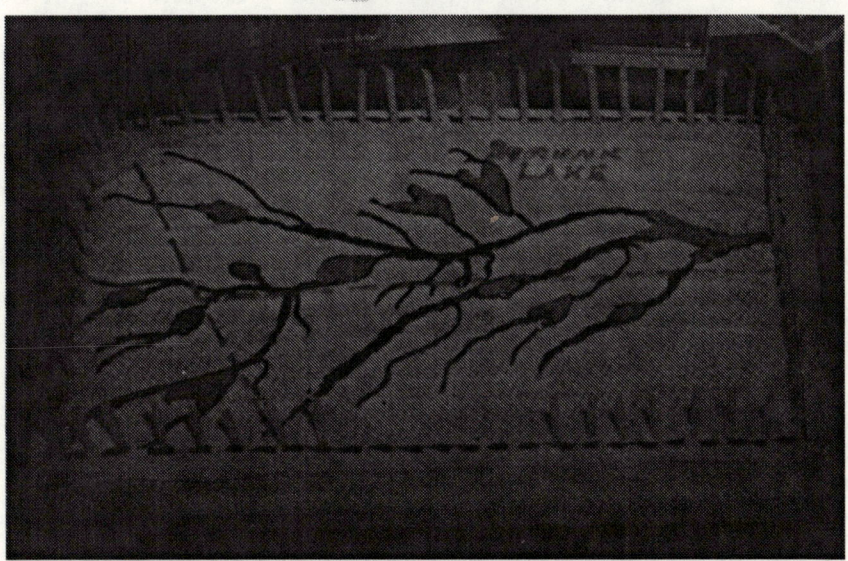

Honored

The map of the Republican River Basin as prepared by the Bureau of Reclamation (top) was reproduced on a cake for Harry Strunk's 62th birthday in 1954 by friends in honor of his untiring lifetime of reclamation work.

Acknowledging Sen. Norris' accomplishment in rural electrification, fair labor legislation, the lame duck amendment, and breaking the Joe Cannon strangle hold on the House, Strunk wrote:

"We contest the decision of the committee which presumes to tell us who are the outstanding senators of this country. We will make up our own minds, will select them ourselves, make our own decisions. And, when we do, in Nebraska we will label Sen. George W. Norris as one of the greatest statesman this country ever produced."

A 1949 article done for the Omaha World-Herald magazine section by McCook writer Doris Minney quoted Strunk as saying "The only difference Sen. Norris and I ever had was that the senator was about 99 percent for development of power. I was about 99 percent for the development of irrigation, flood control and recreation areas."

The article continued to say that the senator, after returning to McCook to retire, had come to Strunk's office and admitted he thought the overall local project was right after all.

Strunk virtually spent a lifetime working for the development of reclamation in the Republican Valley. He dedicated his newspaper to that end and showed a personal determination that was untiring and unbelievable.

"If you want someone to haunt a house, call on Harry Strunk!" That's how Bureau of Reclamation Commissioner Michael Strauss described Strunk's persistence when he addressed one of the many annual meetings of the Republican Valley Conservation Association in McCook.

Strunk's phone calls to Washington bureaucrats came at all times of the day and night and even included the President of the United States.

Retired McCook telephone operator Phyllis Grenier said handling a direct call from Strunk to President Harry S. Truman was a highlight of her career.

"I remember they called each other by first names and Mr. Strunk had the number of the president when he (Truman) was staying at the Waldorf Astoria in New York," she recalled adding she remembers the date being in the late 1940s early 1950s.

And, Truman wasn't the only president that came in direct contact with the Southwest Nebraska personality.

President Dwight D. Eisenhower was invited to come to McCook by Strunk, and Eisenhower accepted. The WWII hero not only visited McCook, but he included five other states.

The idea of the six-state reclamation tour was initiated by Strunk who was quoted in an August 31, 1954 story as saying:

"I was lying in a hospital with my foot broken. There was nothing to do. Just eat and think. It was hot and I kept thinking of the water now stored in the dams and the canals.

"Then I read in the papers where Eisenhower was going to Denver for a vacation when Congress adjourns.

"I thought to myself why not ask him to come out here to see for himself why we need water, where we have built dams, and why we need $100 million more to build the irrigation canals and laterals to put the stored water to use and to provide for additional dams already approved by Congress.

"I thought we should offer him an opportunity to inspect some of our problems out here and learn of them firsthand.

"I called Bud Ryan (RVCA lobbyist in Washington) and asked what he thought of the idea."

Strunk also phoned Don Martin, public relations officer for the Bureau of Reclamation in Denver and son of the associate publisher of the Denver Post. Congressmen and governors in many states were enlisted to support the invitation and thus the proposed tour was enlarged to include the Dakotas, Wyoming, Colorado and Kansas.

Eisenhower's plane flew over many of the states for an aerial inspection without landing, but in Nebraska the "Columbine" sat down at the WWII air base north of McCook and the former general addressed the throngs. A 28-page special edition of the McCook Daily Gazette greeted the president.

Even though President Eisenhower was impressed with the reclamation development in the McCook area and elsewhere, that didn't stop him from dropping the proposed Red Willow Dam in an action six years later in 1960 when in a balanced budget effort he asked Congress for no new reclamation starts.

Twenty Republicans and 260 Democrats voted to override Eisenhower's second "new starts" veto, ending a record of 145 successful vetoes, and giving the final green light to the project 11 miles north of McCook.

Strunk's interest in reclamation dated back to the same year he founded his newspaper – 1911.

"E.B. Bebler, an engineer from Denver, surveyed the Frenchman River that year," Strunk was later quoted as observing.

"It was his (Bebler's) idea that water could be obtained from that river to irrigate upland dry farms to a point as far east as the present site of the former McCook Army Air Base. That's where I probably got my resolve to keep hammering away to get irrigation and flood control," Strunk said.

Another place that drew Strunk's attention to the need for water development and conservation was his home area of Southeast Nebraska. A drought of the early 1900s had been felt in that area killing some of the maple trees on the farm near Pawnee City where Strunk had been born.

Strunk was more than ready for action by 1928 when the Twin Valley Association was formed and he played a major role the following year in organizing the Flood Congress meeting in McCook which drew governors and representatives from 14 states and laid the groundwork for the Pick-Sloan plan for the overall development of the Missouri River Drainage Basin.

It was another decade, however, before the Republican Valley Conservation Association took the place of the defunct Twin Valley group. Strunk became president when the RVCA formed in 1940.

With monthly assessments of $3 per hundred population, approximately two dozen towns in Southwest Nebraska and Northwest Kansas supported the united effort.

Strunk remained the group's elected president until he died in 1960. In 1954, Strunk did resign for a short time to pass the banner to E.H. "Hub" Robinson, who just retired as manager of the McCook office of the Bureau of Reclamation. Robinson served in the job for only a matter of weeks however and the task again fell back to Strunk.

Much of the RVCA's success was credited to Bud Ryan who did an outstanding job of lobbying in Washington. Ryan was from the Dakotas and had a sincere belief in the need for water conservation.

Ryan represented the RVCA for the bargain price of $200 monthly plus expenses and the organization was often in arrears in paying him but he continued to open doors and gain support from Washington officials. Ryan also represented the American Hotel Association and drew most of his livelihood from that group.

On the RVCA Board of Directors, Strunk surrounded himself with some of the most capable and influential men in the area. From McCook he drew close support from Harold Sutton, longtime treasurer of the association, and such others as Roland Larmon, president of the First National Bank; R.G. Stevens of Stevens 7-up; H.C. Clapp of Clapps Store; District Judge Victor Westermark; Don Thompson, who succeeded Strunk, and veterinarian M. Campbell.

Loyal area supporters included P.N. Foster, Imperial; Jake Bauer, Benkelman; Joe Crews, Culbertson; Clarence Benjamin, Arapahoe; Dr. W. Stephenson, Norton, Kan.; Clyde Payne, Edison; George Proud, Arapahoe; Ralph Clark, Oberlin; T.J. Minnick, Cambridge; C.C. Sherwood, Orleans; Don Posstlewaite, St. Francis, Kan.; Carl Swanson, Culbertson, and A.A. Gillespie, St. Francis.

Delayed by the war years, by 1946 it appeared dirt was to begin to fly in Southwest Nebraska's long-awaited development with the beginning of the Enders Reservoir. Then in the fall, President Truman announced a moratorium on public works.

"There was just one day of grace left before it would have been too late to get work started on the Enders schedule, so I began calling about 1:30 p.m. At one time we had on the telephone Sen. Kenneth Wherry, Sen. Hugh Butler, Rep. Carl Curtis, M.O. Ryan and the heads of several government agencies," Strunk said.

"About 5:30 p.m. there came a call from John Steelman, an aide to Truman who said, 'Harry Strunk, I have good news for you. Your contract to go ahead with work on Enders dam was okayed'."

In the years that followed more than $175 million was expended in the construction of Enders Dam, Trenton Dam, Medicine Creek Dam, Bonny Dam, Norton Dam and Red Willow Dam plus several diversion dams and miles of canals and laterals taking water to some 67,000 acres.

Strunk was presented with a bound leather book of letters of commendation signed by President Truman "in recognition of service to reclamation" at the RVCA's annual meeting Sept. 27, 1952. He also received an engraved wristwatch from the RVCA.

The President's award was presented by Sen. Hugh Butler while the watch presentation was made by Hugh Eisenhart, then mayor of Cambridge.

The year before Strunk had been given the U.S. Department of Interior Conservation Service Award and became the first Nebraskan to have his portrait hung in the Bureau of Reclamation Hall of Fame.

Strunk had moved some big mountains. At the time his efforts were only partially appreciated as many of his counterparts leaned back and wrongly concluded the development was automatic and would have taken place anyway. On occasion, he was even bucked by local folks.

One showdown with local powers came in the early 1950s when a money-short McCook Chamber of Commerce led some to conclude the secretarial chamber job and that of the RVCA should be one and the same.

After a series of local Chamber meetings, Strunk told the planners he was keeping his secretary and they could do whatever they liked. That ended the proposed economy move.

Another time, out of pure luck or with the undisclosed help of a never identified telephone operator, Strunk picked up his phone to get in on a conversation between an area banker and a McCook businessman who were raking Strunk over the coals.

"I'm tired of this one-manned Strunk show," one of the two commented drawing general support from his listener.

Obviously both were shocked when Strunk came on the line and volunteered his RVCA presidency to either of the two men. No more criticism came from either of them as the years passed.

If there was one thing Harry Strunk never backed away from, it was controversy. On occasion that even broke into open fisticuffs.

During WWI McCook supported only three gasoline stations, one of which didn't see fit to voluntarily close certain days at the request of the federal government as a gasoline conservation measure. McCook has always had a heavy German population, many of whom left the old country not many years before the war. Many had relatives who remained in Germany and consequently some McCookites weren't totally in accord with American involvement.

Loyalty certainly wasn't all one-sided in McCook, Neb. during those tense times, but there wasn't any question where the Red Willow County Gazette stood.

Strunk editorialized against the station remaining open. Now the station owner outweighed Strunk considerably and was used to physical labor. The first time their paths crossed a few days after the editorial appeared, the gasoline station operator challenged the editor and a fight on Main Street followed.

Effective Team
Sens. Carl Curtis (left) and Roman Hruska were Nebraska's two Republican senators during the period when most of the legislation was passed that advanced reclamation development in Southwest Nebraska and Northwest Kansas. They were both loyal friends and supporters of Harry Strunk and his RVCA cause.

Strunk didn't claim a victory, but did contend he developed a new, and effective wrestling hold that saved him from being pulverized. Strunk got his finger into his opponent's mouth and twisted his opponent's head backward and sideways.

Strunk boasted that he was a graduate from the school of hardknocks and throughout his professional life he was conscious of his limited formal education that had ended with the eighth grade. He always felt he had missed something important about not having a college education and thus insisted his two children go to college.

He also felt he had missed something by having been exempted as critical to business when he was given preferred status during WWI. He had been the second in Red Willow County behind Harold Sutton to register for the draft.

He always maintained a special respect for those in the military and seemed sorry they were part of something he had missed.

When Strunk was born at Pawnee City in 1892, he was last of five children. His father, a captain in the Civil War, was a farmer and had held several county jobs including sheriff.

When Harry Strunk reached the age of 14, his father thought it was time his last son began paying for his own shoes. With this economic situation plus a disagreement with the schoolmaster, young Strunk quit school and took a job on a delivery wagon.

With the exception of an uncle who left Harry Strunk $1,000 in Strunk's later years, and a brother who advised the younger Strunk to "choose your friends rather than letting them choose you," Strunk never inherited anything. But, he felt his father did him a great service in scouting around the town of Pawnee City and getting him lined up as a printer's devil at the local weekly newspaper. The elder Strunk saw more opportunity in that job than in the delivery position even though starting pay was only $2 a week.

After a year's work on the Pawnee City Republican, the young printer was lured to a newspaper at Fairbury, Nebraska by the offer of $7 weekly. However, he returned to his hometown when he learned of the illness of the Pawnee City editor. While the editor was confined to bed for three months, Strunk got his first taste of publishing at the tender age of 16. He was the paper's only employee.

He later jumped south of the Nebraska border and published the Powhatan, Kan., newspaper for a short time for an absentee owner.

He moved west to Norton, Kan., which was his first experience in the daily newspaper field at the Norton Daily Telegram. He was shop foreman in charge of 10 employees (mostly women) who set type by hand. He was only 17 years old.

The ambitious and broke printer was on his way to the West Coast when he passed through Indianola where his brother, John, lived. While there he noticed an ad for a printer at McCook and Strunk hired on to the McCook Tribune before founding his semi-weekly.

Strunk was always progressive in his business outlook and ventured beyond what his banker generally advised. For instance, his was the first newspaper between Hastings and Denver to purchase a linotype, the machine that replaced handset type. He constructed a new building in 1926, two years after going daily and his was one of the first newspapers of its size to utilize teletypesetters, a tape operated version of the linotype. The teletype conversion was made just prior to WWII.

The Hat

With each of the six reservoirs constructed in Southwest Nebraska, Northwest Kansas and Eastern Colorado came the famous dedication ceremonies that brought the national and state political scene to McCook. Barbecues, parades, beauty contests, dinners, music, drama productions and speeches were all part of the pageantry at various times. On this occasion, Strunk left his hat on the speakers' stand while addressing the throngs.

The GAZETTE over the years kicked off several unusual promotional schemes to build itself and the community. Among them were tremendous circulation-building promotions which would feature giving away as many as three new automobiles to successful circulation sales participants. The promotion built readership for the newspaper and also brought in badly needed cash.

One of its most successful continuing community promotions was when the newspaper office served as a collection point for Christmas toys for the less fortunate. It was called the Tiny

Tim Project and it was back in the days before plastic when toys could be repaired and repainted and redistributed.

The most publicized promotion of the GAZETTE came on the eve of the Great Depression when it purchased a 1929 Curtiss Robin airplane and became the first newspaper in the world to regularly deliver newspapers by air.

The GAZETTE employed a pilot by the name of Steve Tuttle from Oberlin, Kan., to initiate the history-making venture that was kicked off with a colossal air show in McCook.

Called the "Newsboy," the airplane flew 389 miles daily dropping newspaper bundles in 46 communities.

A depressed economy and a windstorm that damaged the aircraft put an end to the sensational delivery but created a chapter in journalism and aviation that folks around McCook talked about for years.

The original "Newsboy" was sold after being damaged in the storm and eventually became the property of two TWA pilots who were aviation antique buffs. The plane is now at the Space Museum in Seattle, Wash.

Although Strunk admitted he believed in a Supreme Being, he was not particularly religious. Strunk said a few things happened that made him feel he was getting special help from "upstairs."

One such occurrence happened about a year after he opened the Red Willow County Gazette when machinery and paper supply companies were threatening to reclaim their merchandise due to unpaid bills, and printers were demanding their wages in advance. Strunk received a call one afternoon from a friend at Indianola who said a circulation solicitor was doing a terrific job of selling subscriptions, but he wanted to know how the GAZETTE could sell regular $4 subscriptions for 25 cents. Strunk was dumbfounded. He had no subscription solicitor, and especially not one who was obligating him to deliver a year's subscription at the ridiculous rate of 25 cents per year.

He quickly rented a Model T Ford and went to Indianola where he drove the streets until he spotted a middle-aged woman going from house to house. He confronted her and asked what she was selling.

"Oh, I'm selling subscriptions to the Red Willow County Gazette," she responded. "Would you be interested?"

"Well, how's it going? How many have you sold," he asked.

"I'm having good luck. I must've sold about 45 so far."

"And for whom are you working?"

"Why, sir, I'm working for Jesus Christ," the woman replied.

"Well, he's a very good friend of mine, but I happen to own the paper you're selling for 25 cents a year, and the people you've sold are going to expect me to fulfill this obligation and it can't be done for 25 cents a year," Strunk stated.

"Oh, I'm certainly glad to meet you, Mr. Strunk. I had no idea I was doing you an injustice. You have a fine paper and I wanted to help you, and if you will figure how much those people owe I'll pay the difference," she apologized.

Publisher

In 1926, Harry Strunk moved his newspaper, which had been daily for only two years, from the present Clapp Store to 422 Norris (then called Main Street). The newspaper made journalistic and aviation history in 1929 when it became the first in the world to deliver papers daily by airplane.

She pulled $140 from a role of several hundred dollars and paid the young publisher in $20 bills. He returned to McCook without even asking her name, paid off some debts and continued to publish his newspaper with about 45 new customers.

Harry Strunk had a philosophy all his own. He developed it over the years and cherished three quotes, one of which he had engraved in the stone on the front of his 422 Norris Avenue building.

"Service Is the Rent We Pay for the Space We Occupy in This World," was a part of his newspaper philosophy that he sincerely tried to fulfill during a half-century in the McCook newspaper world.

Although not original, that phrase caused many to think over the years of what responsibility they also had to society and brought many comments to the paper. One Catholic nun teacher used to make an annual trip to the GAZETTE office with her students to observe and reflect on the inscription.

It is still a standing quote in the GAZETTE's masthead and was placed on a plaque at the entrance of the new building constructed at W. First and E in 1966.

Another quote that Strunk admired and one that has always been part of the newspaper's masthead was from Abraham Lincoln. It reads: "Give Us Faith That Right Makes Might and in That Faith Let Us Dare To Do Our Duty As We See It."

During one of the routine resettings of the slogans in type, someone inadvertently used "Fit" instead of "It." The error ran undiscovered for several weeks and finally was spotted by Strunk who quickly had it corrected and disgustedly explained doing duty as "we see fit" is a whole lot different than what Abraham Lincoln meant.

Strunk's third favorite quote was printed on the front of a bookcase in his office and he used it on occasion in his editorials. It read: "On the Plains of Hesitation Bleach the Bones of Unnumbered Thousands Who at the Dawn of Victory Sat Down to Wait and Waiting Died."

Part of Harry Strunk's newspaper philosophy was carried above the nameplate on the front page for a number of years after the paper went daily July 1, 1924. It read: "Dedicated to Carry the Banner of McCook's Ideals."

Another inspirational and unique practice that editor Strunk followed for a number of years included a set of objectives for the newspaper and community which was found daily on the editorial page.

The daily reminders for 1928, for instance, included:

1. Better artery highways.
2. Better local transportation.
   a. Improved rail schedules to conform with the needs of Southwest Nebraska.
   b. Passenger bus lines linking McCook and Southwest Nebraska towns closer together.
3. A definite park program that will assure ample park facilities for the future growth of McCook.
4. A milk inspection ordinance which will be rigidly enforced to guarantee purity in all milk sold in McCook.
5. Construction of a Memorial Auditorium honoring veterans of all wars.

Harry Strunk's philosophy included a touch of human kindness which was always evident in the twinkle in his eye that a few close friends could detect. One of his acts of kindness that left an impression with a few who knew about it involved the purchase of two winter coats for two poorly clad and needy McCook youngsters.

It was a cold wintry day during the Great Depression and a boy of about 12 years of age wearing a badly worn sweater entered the newspaper office. Perhaps seeing himself in need at that age, Harry Strunk invited the lad to accompany him to the Montgomery Ward Store a block away where he made a present to the boy of one of the store's warmest sheep-lined coats.

The grateful boy and Strunk parted as they came out of the store with Strunk returning to his office. He had hardly removed his own coat before the lad reappeared wearing his new coat and accompanied by a younger brother whose need was obviously as great. Strunk made a second trip to the Wards store, this time accompanied by both boys for a second purchase. All three left warmer inside and out.

"He seldom was seen inside a church yet he was more religious than the majority of Sunday worshippers," wrote his son, Allen, in a front-page editorial at the time of the senior Strunk's death in 1960.

"Harry Strunk had a religion all his own and followed it throughout life. He believed in a Supreme Being and living a Christian life. But beyond this and in place of penances and sorrow, he believed working for mankind helped wash out a man's sins. He observed, it isn't how long a man lives, but how he lives. He worked diligently because, like all humans, he had his uncontrollable faults and no one was more aware of them than himself."

Strunk had two children, both of whom he nudged into journalism educations. His daughter, Shirley, was a graduate of the University of Nebraska and worked for short periods on the GAZETTE and the Lincoln Journal. His son, Allen, joined him at the GAZETTE in 1953 after graduating from Northwestern University at Evanston Ill., and serving two years in the Marine Corps.

While at Northwestern, the younger Strunk wrote a personality sketch on his father as a class assignment. The writing was a high point for the senior Strunk and the proud father had copies made and distributed to friends and associates, some of whom were newspaper people and parts of it showed up in such esteemed publications as the Denver Post.

The college student in 1950 wrote in the profile:

> In my opinion, the world's greatest man is not President Truman, General Eisenhower, or Clark Gable, but my ole man.
>
> Dad has a skeleton-like build. Although he is 6 feet 3 inches tall, he weighs only 165 pounds. The deep wrinkles in his face give him a mean, hard look, but his dark blue eyes express a gentle kindness. The large, blunt nose that protrudes from his suntanned face resembles that of an American Indian. He has thick gray hair that was originally black, and wears a hat only during cold weather.
>
> The 57-year-old man can run 15 billiards, hit a pheasant at 50 yards and catch the biggest fish in

the river. And although he also bowls and plays golf, he claims he has no favorite sport.

He likes beer, smokes two packages of cigarettes a day and prefers Scotch whiskey.

He likes his steaks practically raw and responds with a grumble when his potatoes are not mashed. He rarely eats salads or desserts and wouldn't think of eating a cucumber. Because of his false teeth he can't eat corn-on-the-cob and usually trims the ear with a knife, whether he's at home or at the Marine Dining Room of the Edgewater Beach Hotel.

His many friends include industrialists, politicians, farmers and porters all the way from Chicago and Denver. A business associate of my dad's once told me, "When God made your father, he threw away the blueprint because he never made another man with a personality like his."

Dad says his main hobby is people. He likes to know what they think and why. Although he doesn't know the difference between a phobia and a myopia, he claims he is a "damn good psychologist."

He can get into a taxi and before he has ridden a mile, he knows the cab driver's political, social and economic views and sometimes even his personal history.

> When he leaves the bar, he either has one more friend, one more enemy, or some knowledge he didn't have when he entered.

Harry Strunk comes closer to being a legend that anyone who has played a part in the community's first 100 years. The stories about him are numerous.

"In 1930 I was 23 years old when I came to McCook to consider opening a mortuary," recalls Art Herrmann.

"I was married to an acquaintance of Kenneth Wherry. The later-to-become-senator told me to look up his friend Harry Strunk if I needed advice at McCook.

"I visited Strunk's office and said:

"Mr. Strunk, I'm coming to McCook and our mutual friend, Kenneth Wherry, said if I needed any advice out here to look up his friend, Harry Strunk.

"I visited with him a little and told him I was coming to McCook to start a funeral home, and I was wondering just what this territory had to offer.

"He looked at me and asked: 'What do you have to offer McCook?'"

Herrmann, who recently marked more than a half-century in the McCook funeral home business, also tells the story of the time he stopped by the GAZETTE office, which doubled as the RVCA office, when secretary Annette Trimble was taking a call from Harry Strunk.

Strunk was in Chicago and found himself without his false teeth.

Cartoon Humor

Newspaper cartoonist John Somerville, a McCook native, was on the staff of the Denver Post when he had fun with this sketch. Somerville moved on to other metropolitan newspapers and other adventures while Strunk kept plugging away and finally saw dam and canal construction for his efforts.

"Harry was asking Annette to rummage around and find a set of his teeth in his desk drawer. She found a set of his own dentures," Herrmann said.

"I said okay, I'll take care of this. So I took the teeth up to the funeral home and sent them to him with a note saying I'd gone through the assortment of dentures at the funeral home and I do trust these will fit you."

Mrs. Trimble said she also sent a pair but that due to the mail mix-up Strunk was home before his teeth caught up with him.

Strunk's friend Herrmann headed a memorial effort after Strunk's death which resulted in the State Roadside Park along US Highways 6 and 34 two miles east of McCook.

Former McCookite Frank Morrison, then governor, played a key role in securing the funds for the park area and most of the memorial funds came from friends and acquaintances of the long time reclamationist.

"A memorial to Harry D. Strunk, founder and president of the Republican Valley Conservation Association, whose vision and determination led to the harnessing of river valleys in Southwest Nebraska, Northwest Kansas and Eastern Colorado. He fought long and hard for control of waste waters and advancement of soil conservation, wildlife and outdoor recreation," the engraved tribute reads.

It was dedicated by Floyd E. Dominy, U.S. Commissioner of the Bureau of Reclamation, Dec. 5, 1960.

Among the Harry Strunk fans in McCook was one of the community's best storytellers – Bob Hassler.

The retired railroader liked to tell the story of when he used to hang around his brother Frank's Keystone Cigar Store located in what was later the card room of the Townhouse, a retirement center converted from the old Keystone Hotel.

The Cigar Store also sold beer and Harry Strunk would stop by nearly daily.

After one day of facing the trials and tribulations of publishing a daily newspaper in a community where readers often take their newspaper personally, Strunk commented to Hassler:

"My goal in life is to irritate someone every day, and some days I do a whole week's work."

Another story that circulates about Harry Strunk concerns one time he decided to leave by train for Chicago. His pre-World War II vintage car died at the intersection of Norris Avenue and B. With the Zephyr already at the depot, he merely left his car in McCook's busiest intersection and walked the last block.

Harry Strunk, in his later years, could see the fruits of a lifetime of work. He had seen the dam construction and irrigation water flowing to dry acres. He saw the beginning of its economic impact and the recreational potential it offered.

But one of the major projects ... the closest to McCook of them all ... one that had been among the first approved for feasibility still remained only on paper through the decades of the 1940s and 1950s.

Red Willow, 11 miles north of McCook, had been approved as part of the original Pick-Sloan Plan. It was given feasibility approval by President Truman in the war year of 1944.

All these favorable actions had been taken, but no Red Willow Dam construction. Enders Dam, Trenton Dam, Medicine Creek Dam and Bonny Dam had been built. But not Red Willow. All work above Harlan County Dam had been given to the Bureau of Reclamation except Red Willow which had been planned as an Army Engineers Project.

After years of political maneuvering, the Red Willow Dam project was traded by the Army Engineers to the Bureau and it was four more years before the project was reapproved by Washington.

"I want to live long enough to see Red Willow built," Strunk said on more than one occasion.

On July 4, 1960, with all the fanfare that had marked other construction starts, groundbreaking was held for another reclamation milestone in the area, and Red Willow Dam was begun.

One month and one day later, Harry Strunk died at St. Catherine's Hospital.

Harry Strunk had seen his last dream come true and had even personally selected a date for the ground-breaking ceremony.

When the committee planning the ceremony met there was some doubt expressed over using the July 4 date since some felt it might be too warm and that families would be involved in other activities over the holiday. To which Strunk said, "okay, have it any day you want...just as long as it's on the fourth of July."

Memorial

Floyd E. Dominy, Commissioner of the Bureau of Reclamation, dedicated the Harry D. Strunk Memorial Rest Area two miles east of McCook at ceremonies Dec. 5, 1960. A map and an inscription recognizing Strunk's reclamation efforts was unveiled at the event. Art Herrmann (standing left) was a key figure in obtaining the memorial.

Printed in the United States
98987LV00005B/253-498/A